Think, Think, Think

WRITTEN BY PAMELA HILL NETTLETON
ILLUSTRATED BY BECKY SHIPE

Thanks to our advisers for their expertise, research, and advice:
Angela Busch, M.D., All About Children Pediatrics, Minneapolis, Minnesota

Susan Kesselring, M.A., Literacy Educator
Rosemount-Apple Valley-Eagan (Minnesota) School District

PICTURE WINDOW BOOKS
MINNEAPOLIS, MINNESOTA

Managing Editor: Bob Temple
Creative Director: Terri Foley
Editor: Kristin Thoennes Keller
Editorial Adviser: Andrea Cascardi
Copy Editor: Laurie Kahn
Designer: Melissa Voda
Page production: The Design Lab
The illustrations in this book were rendered digitally.

Picture Window Books
1710 Roe Crest Drive
North Mankato, MN 56003
www.capstonepub.com

Library of Congress Cataloging-in-Publication Data
 Nettleton, Pamela Hill.
  Think, think, think: learning about your brain / by Pamela Hill Nettleton ;
illustrated by Becky Shipe.
    p. cm. — (The amazing body)
Summary: An introduction to the parts of the brain and how they function.
Includes bibliographical references and index.
  ISBN 978-1-4048-0252-0 (hardcover)
  ISBN 978-1-4048-0503-3 (paperback)
1. Brain—Juvenile literature. [1. Brain.] I. Shipe, Becky, 1977– ill. II. Title.
  QP376 .N465 2004
  612.8'2—dc22   2003018183

What could you do without your brain?
Nothing! Your brain is the big boss of your body!

Your brain controls your thoughts, movements, and feelings. It's like a computer that fits right between your ears!

Your brain takes up the top half of your head.
Your brain is soft, wrinkled, and gray.

Can you lift a jug of milk? Then you can lift an adult-sized brain. It weighs about 3 pounds (1.36 kilograms).

MATH

SCIENCE

ENGLISH

Your brain is made up of three main parts.
Each has a big job—and a big name.

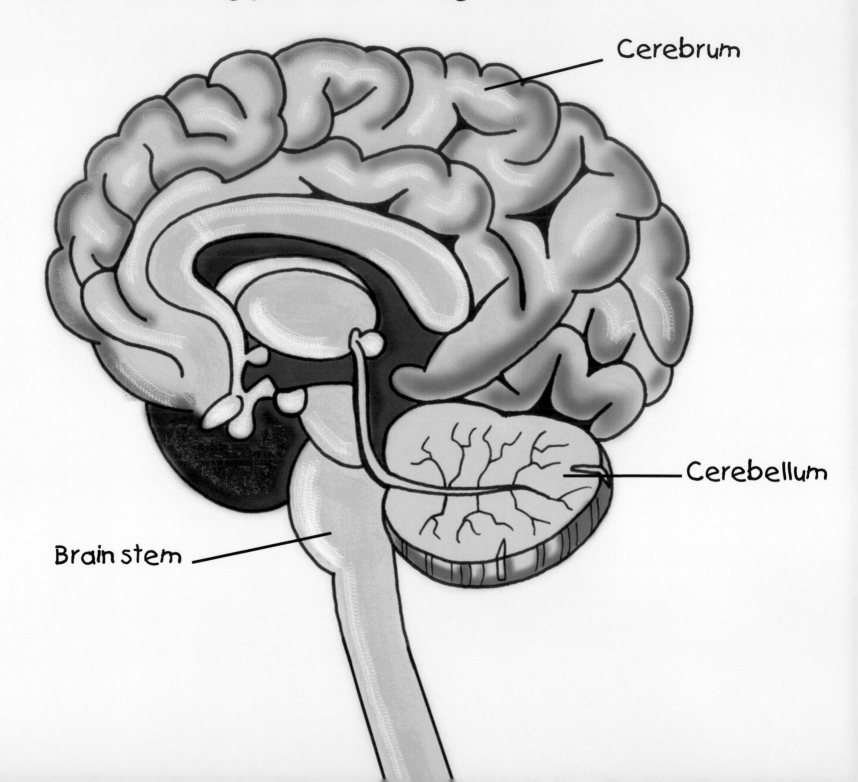

Cerebrum

Cerebellum

Brain stem

The largest part of your brain is called the cerebrum. This is the part that thinks. You use it to figure out problems at school. You use it to make a plan for the day.

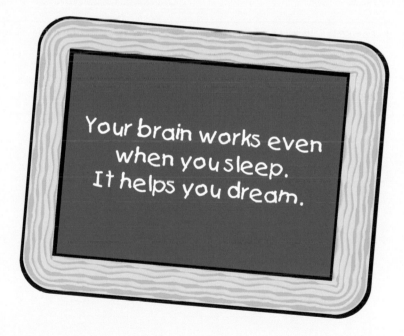

Your brain works even when you sleep. It helps you dream.

The cerebrum has two halves, a right half and a left half. The right half controls the left side of your body. The left half controls the right side of your body.

The right side of your brain helps you play music, draw, and be creative. The left side helps you read and do math.

Across both halves, from ear to ear, is the motor area. This area of the brain helps you move your muscles. You can run, jump, and sink a basket!

The second main part of your brain is called the cerebellum. It's in the back of your head.

The cerebellum helps you balance. It helps you stand. It helps your muscles work together.

If you're an athlete, you really need your cerebellum. You couldn't walk on a balance beam or kick a soccer ball without one.

The third main part of your brain is your brain stem. It connects the rest of your brain to your spinal cord. Your spinal cord goes down your neck and back.

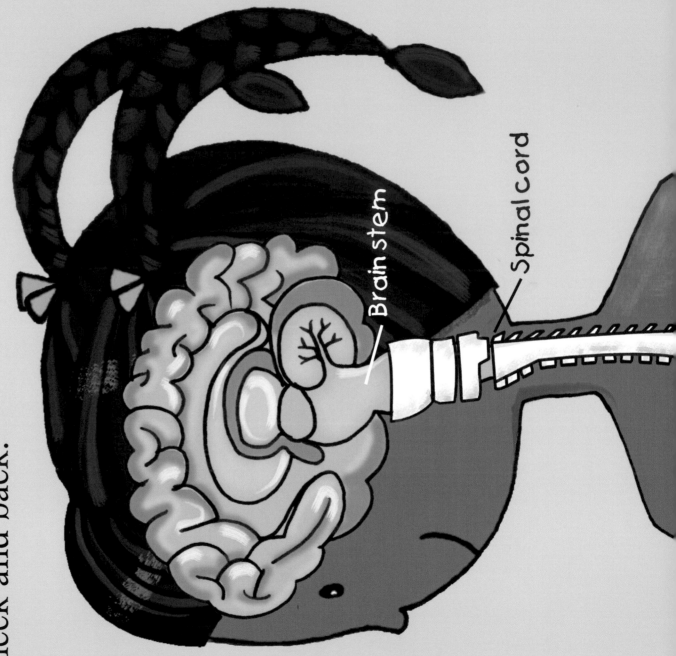

Brain stem

Spinal cord

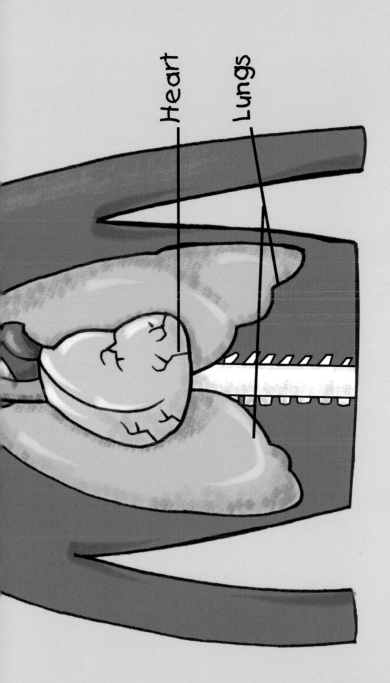

Heart

Lungs

Your brain learns a lot during your first six years. During that time, your brain learns faster than at any other time in your life.

You keep breathing even when you don't think about it. That's your brain stem at work. It keeps your heart beating and your lungs working!

Your brain also contains many little parts
that have big jobs. One part gives off chemicals
that tell your body how big and tall to grow.
Another helps you remember things,
such as what you read in this book.

7 years

years

5 years

4 years

Right in the middle of your brain is a sort of thermostat called a hypothalamus. It tells you when to shiver or sweat.

Your hypothalamus is the part of your brain that keeps your body at 98 degrees Fahrenheit (37 degrees Celsius).

Your brain has a small group of cells on each side called the amygdala. These cells control your feelings. They help you feel sad when you lose a baseball game.

They make you feel happy
when you see your grandpa.

If you bump your head really hard, you might get a concussion. This brain injury happens when the brain knocks against the inside of the skull. You might lose your memory for a while, vomit, or have a bad headache.

Keep your brain safe! Wear a helmet or headgear when playing rough games or riding your bicycle.

Doctors who work with brains are called neurologists.

What makes your brain healthy? Getting enough sleep and eating right are helpful to your brain.

Smoking, drinking alcohol, and using illegal drugs are bad for your brain.

Learning and asking questions are good for your brain. So are reading books and figuring out problems. Thinking is good for you! Keep on using your brain!

THE BRAIN

The three main parts of your brain are the cerebrum, the cerebellum, and the brain stem. The cerebrum helps you think. The cerebellum helps you move. The brain stem keeps your heart and lungs working.

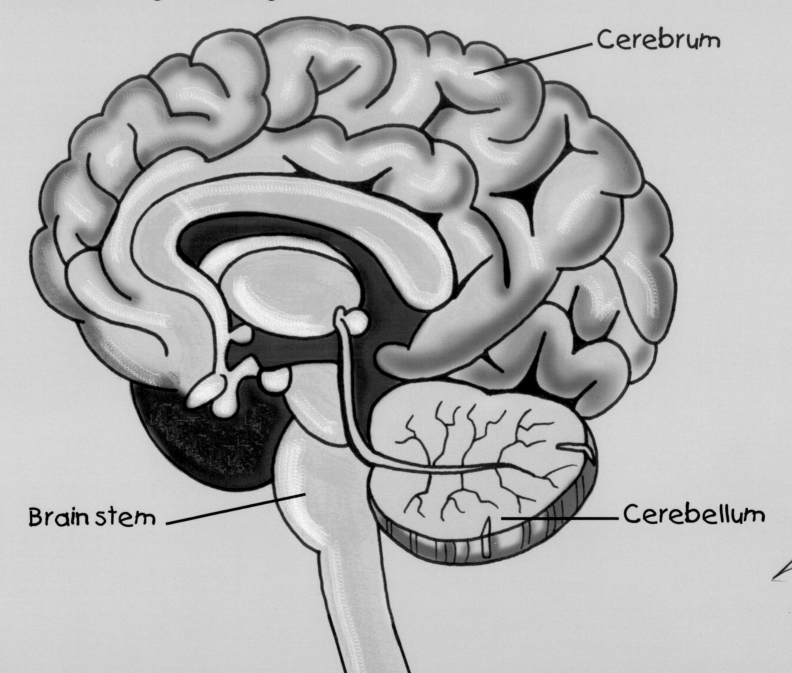

Cerebrum

Brain stem

Cerebellum

USE YOUR OTHER HAND!

What hand do you use to draw, your right or your left? Put a crayon in the hand you usually don't use. Now try to draw a picture. Try to write your name. Try to write your friend's name. One side of your body usually is stronger than the other. Doctors do not know for sure why people end up right-handed or left-handed.

TOOLS OF THE TRADE

Doctors who treat brain problems often use a test called an EEG. It helps measure activity in the brain. Small metal disks are attached to a person's head. These disks have wires attached to them. The wires connect to a machine. The machine reads patterns of activity in the brain. Then the machine prints those results on a sheet of paper for the doctor to read.

A doctor also might use other tests besides an EEG. An MRI and a CT scan use computers to take pictures of the brain.

GLOSSARY

amygdala (uh-MIG-duh-luh)—small groups of cells in your brain that are responsible for your feelings

brain stem (BRAYN STEM)—the part of your brain that connects to your spinal cord

cells (SELZ)—the building blocks of every part of your body. You only can see them with a microscope.

cerebellum (SAIR-uh-bel-uhm)—a small part of the back of the brain that helps you balance and move

cerebrum (suh-REE-bruhm)—a large part of your brain that helps you think

concussion (kuhn-KUSH-uhn)—a brain injury that happens when your brain knocks against the inside of your skull

hypothalamus (hye-puh-THAL-uh-muhss)—your brain's thermostat

neurologist (noo-RAW-luh-jist)—a doctor who treats the brain

TO LEARN MORE

At the Library

Ballard, Carol. *How Do We Think?* Austin, Tex.: Raintree Steck-Vaughn, 1998.

DeGezelle, Terri. *Your Brain.* Mankato, Minn.: Bridgestone Books, 2002.

Furgang, Kathy. *My Brain.* New York: PowerKids Press, 2001.

On the Web

FactHound offers a safe, fun way to find Web sites related to topics in this book. All of the sites on FactHound have been researched by our staff.

1. Visit *www.facthound.com*
2. Type in this special code: 1404802525
3. Click the FETCH IT button.

Your trusty Fact Hound will fetch the best sites for you!

INDEX